P9-DID-754

STEPHEN CHBOSKY

STEPHEN CHBOSKY

PHILIP WOLNY

ROSEN
PUBLISHING®

New York

Published in 2015 by The Rosen Publishing Group, Inc.
29 East 21st Street, New York, NY 10010

First Edition

Library of Congress Cataloging-in-Publication Data

Wolny, Philip.
Stephen Chbosky/Philip Wolny.—First edition.
    pages cm.—(All About the Author)
Includes bibliographical references and index.
ISBN 978-1-4777-7910-1 (library bound)
1. Chbosky, Stephen—Juvenile literature. 2. Novelists, American—20th century—Biography—Juvenile literature. 3. Screenwriters—United States—Biography—Juvenile literature. I. Title.
PS3553.H3469Z94 2015
813'.54—dc23
[B]

2014020383

Manufactured in China

CONTENTS

It was September 2012, and Stephen Chbosky had just sat down with a group of journalists. This was no ordinary group of reporters, but a collection of seven students from various high schools, armed with pens and paper and recording devices, gathered for a rare opportunity to interview a young-adult literature legend. Although a novel experience for the teenagers, for Chbosky it was just the kind of audience he was used to: year after year he had been capturing the imaginations of a continuing stream of young readers with his 1999 book, *The Perks of Being a Wallflower.*

In the interview with these budding journalists of *Blueprint Magazine* (which took place at Pinnacle High School in Phoenix, Arizona), Chbosky spoke about his career as an author, screenwriter, and film director. He put the group at ease, seeming to connect easily with them, much as his literary voice has connected with countless readers over the years. These young reporters scribbled down his words and recorded them with their iPhones.

Over the course of his career, Chbosky has gained a legion of fans that are more dedicated than most. One of the teen journalists present told him that a few students she knew had even taken lines from the novel and had them

Author and filmmaker Stephen Chbosky is pictured here at the Twenty-Fifth Annual Scripter Awards at the University of Southern California, February 9, 2013.

tattooed on their bodies. Others had simply memorized lines from the book. Still others had used the book as a life raft of sorts, reading it to feel less lonely while facing the usual, often isolating growing pains of adolescence. His story validated their experiences.

Chbosky had made his own journey from being a shy and withdrawn junior high schooler to becoming a celebrated writer and filmmaker, as well as the cocreator of a beloved television drama. On the way, however, he never forgot where came from. He had overcome pain and loneliness and had tried his hand at many different kinds of writing. The author maintained a sense of wonder and hope, and he had a few lucky breaks, too. Most important, Chbosky had done his best to learn as much from the mentors whom he encountered and to take to heart the lessons they offered him.

That September day he recounted a story to the teen journalists about the first time he realized what creativity meant, a memory he had also shared with *Blueprint Magazine*. It took place in fourth grade, when his classroom teacher gave out writing assignments, instructing the students to draw covers for their stories. Without even reading or hearing the story, he was struck by a fellow student's horror-story cover. "That was the first inclination I had that books just didn't appear—that people actually created them." On the last day of school that year, he recited a tale about how a killer whale stops a serial killer, which he titled "Two Killers in Snug Harbor." Chbosky laughed, recalling how "it was a terrible story, but it was so sweet that she asked me to read it, and ever since then I thought I could do this. I owe a lot to [her]." From that point on, Stephen Chbosky was on his way to becoming a writer. This is his story.

CHILDHOOD AND IMAGINATION

Stephen Chbosky was born January 25, 1970, in Pittsburgh, Pennsylvania, to Lea Chbosky (formerly Lea Meyer) and Fred G. Chbosky. His hometown, nicknamed "Steel City," had been a longtime center of the steel industry, and young Stephen never quite forgot the stories of his steelworker grandfather looking for work during the Great Depression of the 1930s. Fred Chbosky worked as an executive, chief finance officer, and consultant for steel companies, while his mother was a tax preparer. His family heritage was a combination of Polish, Slovak, Irish, and Scottish, a blend of some of the many groups that helped build Pittsburgh.

The city of Pittsburgh, Pennsylvania, the state's second largest metropolis, is shown here in an archival photo. Pittsburgh has figured heavily in Chbosky's work.

Stephen grew up in the comfortable Pittsburgh suburb of Upper St. Clair. Like many future novelists and screenwriters, Chbosky was a reader and film fan before he was a writer. Stephen first started writing—and fell in love with the craft—while he was a student at Streams Elementary School.

In September 2012, Chbosky revealed to *Script Magazine* that in 1982, when he was twelve years old, "I told my Dad I wanted to be a writer. And he said, 'That's great.' Great writers are great readers.'" Chbosky laughed recalling this exchange because it wouldn't be until his teen years that he would become an avid reader. At the age of twelve, "I didn't read anything . . . I watched HBO nonstop and that's where my love for film began." Some of his favorites were science-fiction epics such as *Star Wars* and comedies such as *The Bad News Bears* and *Meatballs.* Many of his favorite films were about underdogs and lovable losers.

AN AVID READER

Later, when the reading bug kicked in, his favorite books included F. Scott Fitzgerald's first book, *This Side of Paradise*, as well as Fitzgerald's famous *The Great Gatsby*, the tale of a wealthy yet troubled man with humble beginnings. Other favorites of Stephen's were Jack Kerouac's *On the Road* and the plays of Tennessee Williams.

J. D. Salinger's *The Catcher in the Rye* affected Stephen deeply. A coming-of-age story narrated by an earnest but angry young man, Holden Caulfield, it has been a favorite of young readers for generations, and its narrator has become synonymous with teenage rebellion and alienation. It was Salinger with whom later critics would most closely identify Chbosky's future breakthrough work.

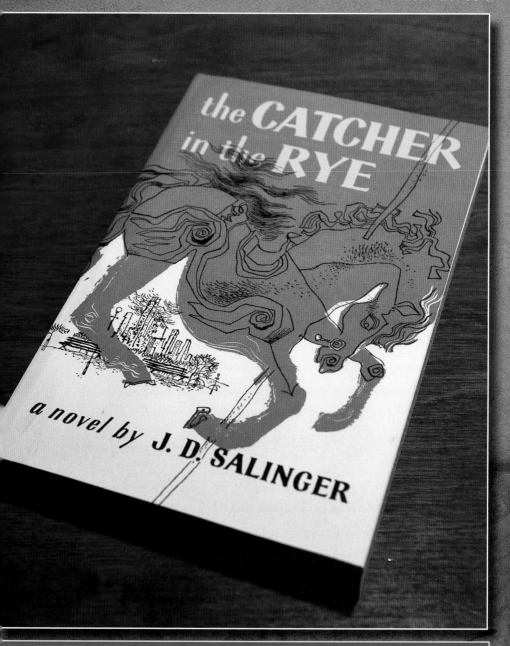

J. D. Salinger's *The Catcher in the Rye* was one of the formative works that influenced Chbosky. Its themes of adolescent longing and alienation affected Chbosky deeply, as it did with successive generations of readers, especially young people who identified with it.

Stephen seemed to favor books about self-discovery and personal development or outsiders overcoming some kind of hardship. He told *L.A. Youth* teen interviewer Ann Beisch, "In terms of the books I liked as a teen, I enjoyed a good blend of the classics, horror, and fantasy. My favorites were *The Great Gatsby*, *To Kill a Mockingbird*, *Death of a Salesman*, *The Shining*, *The Hobbit,* and *Hamlet*."

Stephen's own experiences and sense of himself in his youth influenced some of the characters he would later invent and write about. He was withdrawn, especially during the years when others were becoming social. As he told *Script Magazine*, "There were certain years I remembered very well. I remember in 7th grade, I was painfully shy and didn't venture out of my shell very often, even though I desperately wanted to."

ENGAGING WITH THE WORLD

One teacher who influenced Stephen, and who years later still remembered the young man fondly, especially when he turned up to direct a movie in his hometown, was Mary Lou Einloth. Stephen took Einloth's filmmaking class during his sophomore year of high school. It was an advanced class for him, since it was an elective mostly for seniors and some more advanced juniors.

Einloth told the *Pittsburgh Post-Gazette* in late 2012 how Chbosky worked on animation, including a video of a teddy bear dancing on a bottle. He also tried acting that year, volunteering for the role of a vampire rising from a coffin for a classmate's horror film. Einloth remembered Stephen Chbosky as a genuinely nice and bright young man.

Stephen later came out of his shell. During junior year, he auditioned for all of the musicals that Upper St. Clair High School put on. Besides enjoying them, he realized that it was good to take part because all of the girls he liked performed in them. The musicals were one good way for this wallflower to participate. "It's how I got to be part of the art crowd," he later explained to *Script Magazine.*

A NEW MENTOR

An event toward the end of his high school career, however, would truly cement his future as a writer. Stephen was touring colleges when he visited the University of Southern California (USC), which is well known for its film school. He attended a lecture by screenwriter Stewart Stern. Stern had written and cowritten Hollywood films from the 1950s through the 1970s, including *The Ugly American*, starring the cinematic superstar Marlon Brando. His most famous achievement, however, was writing one of

Screenwriter Stewart Stern wrote the screenplay for the immensely influential *Rebel Without a Cause* (1955). James Dean, pictured here, played the lead role and became a superstar.

Stephen's favorite films, *Rebel Without a Cause*, starring James Dean. The tale of teenage rebellion and alienation was perhaps the first of its kind, and it made Dean into a film legend. Stern's scripts were well known for their sensitive and psychologically complex portrayals of conflicted people.

Listening to Stern's stories about screenwriting and interacting with well-known icons of the film industry hooked young Stephen. He later told USC's *Daily Trojan*, "I'm a 17-year-old kid from Pittsburgh who doesn't know anybody and suddenly I'm listening to this man at USC talk about how he met James Dean and would travel with Marlon Brando. And Paul Newman is his best friend."

He told *Script Magazine*, "I was so impressed by him that I just said to myself, 'If this man is teaching at this school, I'm going to this school.'" The aspiring film student soon kept this promise to himself. Stephen graduated Upper St. Clair High School. Shortly after, he enrolled at USC film school to pursue a bachelor of fine arts in film.

AN EARLY INFLUENCE: *DEAD POETS SOCIETY*

When Chbosky was nineteen years old, he saw *Dead Poets Society*, written by Tom Schulman. It starred Robin Williams as an English teacher at a prep school who mentors and inspires the young men he teaches through poetry and life lessons. Chbosky loved this coming-of-age story. He wrote Schulman a fan letter. To his surprise, Schulman wrote back to him. Chbosky told *Written By: The Journal of the Writers Guild of America* in 2012, "Every generation of young people needs to know that adults respect them and that they're not alone." Schulman's screenplay had conveyed that message to the aspiring screenwriter and author, much as Stern's *Rebel Without a Cause* had to a previous generation, Chbosky observed.

In the 1989 film *Dead Poets Society*, Robin Williams, shown here, portrays John Keating, a poetry teacher at an elite prep school who challenges and inspires his teenage students.

AN ANONYMOUS LETTER

In 1993, Stewart Stern suffered a major heart attack that put him out of commission for a long while. Still the sensitive high schooler at heart, Chbosky was concerned for his newfound mentor, but he did not want to look as though he was coming on too strong or that he was trying to gain some kind of influence with him. He avoided identifying himself to Stern then because "I didn't want [Stern] to think that I was just trying to get him to help me with an agent or something," he told *Written By* magazine.

In the end, Chbosky sent an anonymous letter telling Stern simply, "I just want you to know you changed my life." Chbosky told the *Daily Trojan* that he felt extreme gratitude to Stern because "USC was such a great place for me." He even included a mix tape—a collection of songs by different artists picked by Chbosky—with the letter.

Although Chbosky says it took him about a year and a half, Stern eventually figured out the identity of this mystery letter writer. His gratitude and curiosity eventually brought the teacher and student closer, and Stern became an important mentor to Chbosky.

ORIGINS OF A WALLFLOWER'S VISION

Chbosky took the advice of a few professors and friends, including Stern, and sat down to write a novel, even though he had little experience writing fictional prose. He had recently gone through a bad breakup, and he was writing almost as a type of therapy when inspiration struck. "I was writing a very different type of book," Chbosky admitted to *L.A. Youth*, a now-defunct newspaper by and about Los Angeles teens. His novel's main character was both angry and outgoing, unlike Chbosky through much of his school years. While that particular book never quite took off, a sentence uttered by one of the characters would give wings to another book. The line? "That's one of the perks of being a wallflower."

"I wrote that line," he told *L.A. Youth.* "And stopped. And I realized that somewhere in that title—the perks of being a wallflower—was the kid I was really trying to find. I stopped writing the book I was working on." He did not return to that story or expand upon the new idea he had just yet. It was not the end of the wallflower idea—it just wasn't the time for it yet.

The bronze statue officially known as the Trojan Shrine portrays USC's mascot, Tommy Trojan, and can be seen at the center of the prestigious school's campus.

HITTING THE BIG TIME

Chbosky graduated from USC as part of the class of 1992 during an exciting and innovative era in cinema, especially for independent filmmaking. It was an environment where indie films and their directors flourished, including such talents as Quentin Tarantino, Spike Lee, Steven Soderbergh, and many others. It seemed as though everyone was looking for the "next big thing," and filmmakers with even small budgets could make it big if they had an interesting story to tell.

Chbosky would spend the next few years pursuing his dreams in the film industry. Still, the idea, perhaps simply only a feeling now and not even a story of what would later become his most famous work, lingered for him.

TWO

CHAPTER

THE PERKS OF WRITING A NOVEL

Chbosky began working as a screen-writer, and he had his ups and downs in the film industry. In 1996, at the age of twenty-six, the half-formed ideas and powerful feelings that percolated when he first thought of the title "The Perks of Being a Wallflower" began to take shape in his mind. It had been five years since they had first come to him.

Once again, stress seemed to ignite the spark of literary inspiration. In *Written By*, the author described his feelings around this time: "I was going through a hard time, and I wanted to understand why good people let themselves get treated so badly . . . I wanted to believe that there could still be such a things as a pure soul, and I wanted to look at my upbringing in Pittsburgh and make some peace with it." Chbosky has

Chbosky is shown here arriving at the New York City premiere of the musical film *Rent* at the Ziegfeld Theater on November 17, 2005. Chbosky's screenplay for the film was based on the popular stage musical of the same name.

said to various media outlets that he almost had a mental breakdown during this time of his life.

One Saturday morning, it was as if the main character of the book, Charlie, actually appeared to him. During a video interview with film vloggers DP/30, Chbosky said, "It was like Charlie tapped me

Celebrated since 1995, World Book Night was developed by the United Nations Educational, Scientific, and Cultural Organization (UNESCO) as a way to promote reading and writing.

World Book Night April 23

on the shoulder [and said], 'It's time. You've thought about it enough. Here it comes.'"

The arrival of Charlie's voice felt so real to him. In November 2013, during World Book Night, a gathering of book lovers who volunteer and donate books to those who don't normally read, he described that voice to interviewer Laura Peraza. "It felt like an old friend. I poured all of my memories, thoughts, hopes, dreams, and passions through that voice," he said. He started with the famous "Dear Friend" beginning, and the words began to come. He drew on inspirations from his own young life and from the scenes he had pictured during those five years. "I kept picturing this boy and his two friends and the tunnel and those moments when we feel so alive," he told Peraza, referencing a now-famous scene where the characters drive a pickup truck through a Pittsburgh-area tunnel.

WRITING *PERKS*

Writing *Perks* was an intense emotional experience for the young writer, who actually wrote the novel in two sections. After about a month, Chbosky had half the book. He found, however, that the intensity of the emotions the writing brought out was nearly overwhelming. He admitted to DP/30, "Charlie's voice, it started to get to me a little bit. I needed some distance. I took . . . six months off and then spent six weeks writing it." Chbosky finally had a first draft.

The narrator and main protagonist, Charlie, is a young man beginning his freshman year of high school in a suburb just outside of Pittsburgh, Pennsylvania, a detail lifted from Chbosky's own life. Charlie uses a series of letters addressed to a friend as a personal diary and journal. These writings allow him to express feelings and relate personal events that he might not have shared with anyone out loud.

Over the course of the book, Charlie makes friends and begins to date. He also stands up for himself, faces unrequited (unreciprocated) love, and deals with family relationships. He also has to confront some dark family secrets and come to terms with the trauma of recovering from the deaths of important people in his life. As is the case with many coming-of-age novels, *Perks* tells a story of how a character changes and grows, even if he must go through great difficulties to do so.

CHARLIE VS. STEPHEN

Much of the novel came from Chbosky's own teen years, though the book was not fully autobiographical. Even some of his college-era experiences influenced certain plot points, including a few of the characters. His real era of being a wallflower occurred when he was in seventh grade, during which he later admitted he was extremely withdrawn. He told

AN EPISTOLARY NOVEL

The novel Chbosky wrote can be described as an epistolary work. This word has its origins in the Greek *epistolē*, meaning "message," "dispatch," or "letter." This kind of novel or work is written in the format of a series of fictional documents. Epistolary novels usually take the form of a series of letters written from one character to another or letters exchanged between and among various characters. Other documents might include excerpts of books, newspaper articles, and other sources. One of Chbosky's favorite authors, Stephen King, first achieved massive success with his epistolary coming-of-age horror tale *Carrie*. In *The Perks of Being a Wallflower*, Charlie is the letter-writing narrator reaching out to another, unknown and anonymous student, to whom he refers only as a friend, with the salutation "Dear."

several media outlets that he barely left his room if he did not have to during that troubled year.

Other elements of Chbosky's life made it into the book, too, albeit often in a completely altered form. One of Charlie's new friends his freshman year, who becomes a major character in the book, is Patrick, a gay senior secretly having an affair with a member of the football team. While he did not know someone like him in high school, Patrick was actually based

Matthew Broderick starred as the title character in the 1986 film *Ferris Bueller's Day Off*, about a popular and rebellious high schooler.

on Chbosky's gay friend at USC, who first introduced the college student to the gay community. Patrick is also partly based on the eponymous hero of the 1986 John Hughes film *Ferris Bueller's Day Off*.

In addition, Patrick's stepsister Sam, a character influenced by one of Chbosky's own high school crushes, becomes the object of Charlie's affections. His mentor Stewart Stern provided some of the inspiration for Bill, Charlie's English teacher, who notices something special in the novel's hero and attempts to encourage his love of reading and writing.

A POP-CULTURAL SMORGASBORD

Chbosky's novel is chock-full of his own literary, cinematic, and musical influences. Many of these sources have coming-of-age themes, or have been popular with young people throughout the decades. Among the books included are Salinger's *The Catcher in the Rye*, Fitzgerald's *The Great Gatsby*, Harper Lee's *To Kill a Mockingbird*, and *A Separate Peace* by John Knowles. Films mentioned in the novel include *The Rocky Horror Picture Show*, *Dead Poets Society*, and *The Graduate*. Chbosky also mentions and quotes 1980s music, classic rock, and 1990s alternative rock. Musical artists featured in *Perks* include Simon and Garfunkel, Fleetwood Mac, Pink Floyd, Genesis, U2, Nirvana, and Smashing Pumpkins, among others. For many readers, these minor flourishes give the story extra depth and impact. They also provide reference points for those readers who were coming of age when the book came out.

A promotional photo of musicians Paul Simon and Art Garfunkel. Referenced in Chbosky's novel, the now-defunct duo's music has exemplified the joy and pain of growing up for listeners from the 1960s through today.

NOVEL WRITING AS THERAPY

Chbosky hoped that the book would connect with others, but this would-be response had not been his primary influence in writing it. Chbosky told USC's *Daily Trojan*, "I wasn't really thinking about the reader then . . . I was just thinking about Charlie and what he was going through and trying to answer the question for myself and why good people let themselves get treated so badly." *Perks* was the author's answer to that question, and it has given him great satisfaction that the novel has helped other readers answer that question for themselves, applying its message to their own lives.

Chbosky's story later became known for its sincere depiction of teenage love, alienation, coping, and growth, which include some frank portrayals of drug use and sexual relations. The author perhaps did not realize exactly how big an impact his very personal story would have, however. *Perks* would soon touch many lives, and in the process, change Chbosky's own. Before any of that, however, the author would have to get his book published.

SHOPPING A NOVEL

The story of *Perks*'s journey from Chbosky's imagination to new literary sensation happened because of the author's own hard work, the connections he had made in the film industry during and since his studies at USC, and sheer, dumb luck. For about two years, he shopped around his manuscript, with little success.

Christopher McQuarrie, the writer of the cult crime drama *The Usual Suspects*, and who later worked on films such as *The Tourist*, *Jack Reacher*, and *Jack the Giant Slayer*, had been Chbosky's advisor during a screenwriting program at the Sundance Institute. Chbosky had written a script then, but it, too, had gone nowhere. McQuarrie later joked to *Written By*, "I was of no use to him as an advisor. We spent our time watching cable TV in my room. We never did discuss his script."

McQuarrie's friendship with Chbosky did come into play, however. Chbosky had made little headway with literary agents or publishers. But he sent McQuarrie the novel. In 1998, McQuarrie was at an airport reading it when one line affected him deeply: "We accept the love we think we deserve."

Inspired, McQuarrie thought back to a woman he had met named Heather Neely. Initially, he thought he had no chance with her. But the line, and Chbosky's manuscript, energized him, influencing him to try to date her. McQuarrie and Neely eventually married. It was a real-life twist that Chbosky might have written.

Neely, in turn, would prove useful to Chbosky. Neely had gone to college with a man named Eduardo Braniff. Braniff was the head of the recently established MTV Books, a publishing house started by the influential video and media television network. Things moved fast then, and within six weeks, Chbosky had signed on with a literary agent, Jack Horner. Most important, Braniff and MTV Books had offered him a deal. The book came out on February 19, 1999.

AN INSTANT CLASSIC

Chbosky, his publishers, his agent, and other readers knew they had something special in their hands. Teenage readers latched on to the emotional honesty and poignant themes of loss, growing up, friendship, and slighted romance. Many identified closely with Charlie especially because he had such a problem connecting with others. His journey toward self-acceptance and dealing with his problems gave them hope and catharsis—a way to feel deep emotions through the struggles of a fictional character.

The Perks of Being a Wallflower began to gain cult status. Over the coming years, through the 2000s, and into the present, it has sold hundreds of thousands of copies. Perks also gained a kind

Chbosky's debut novel, *The Perks of Being a Wallflower*, has achieved a readership of millions, far beyond the amount of copies sold because of it being widely circulated among classmates and friends.

of popularity that left Chbosky even more satisfied and fulfilled: word-of-mouth exchange among teenage readers. Its sensitive depiction of teenage life made it a popular book for avid readers to lend to their friends.

Tara Aquino, interviewing Chbosky for Complex.com in 2012, declared that the book had "saved lives" due to its ability to connect to readers so personally. Chbosky told Complex.com that fans often approached him with stories about how the book helped them feel less alone, if only for a short while or just while reading it. The more he heard such accounts, the less alone in the world Chbosky felt, too. "Now I feel more connected to people than I ever have," he said.

Chbosky also told interviewer John Hanlon how deeply some teens' reactions to his novel had affected him. "Some letters I received over the years will rip your heart," he said. "This is the quote I remember more than anything else. One girl wrote to me, 'The first time that I ever felt loved was reading your book.' That'll change you." Chbosky was even contacted by one teen who said the book saved her from committing suicide at age fourteen, while the friend of a suicidal seventeen-year-old reported that the boy had read the book and backed off from a similar tragic decision.

COURTING CONTROVERSY

With its frank depictions of sexuality, homosexuality, drugs, suicide, abuse, and other sensitive topics, it was inevitable that Chbosky's book would gain some notoriety, even as it gained a legion of devoted fans. Two school districts within the United States banned it successfully—in Massachusetts and New York's Long Island—while in 2004, a group of parents in Wisconsin unsuccessfully challenged its place in the school curriculum. Protests by readers and free-speech advocates made a compelling case, however, and the school board there rejected the ban. Chbosky even wrote them a letter defending his work and the rights of young people to read it.

Having grown up a Roman Catholic, Chbosky was sympathetic to those people who felt threatened by the book's themes. But he felt their criticism was shortsighted, especially since parents and students had the right to read an alternate title if it conflicted with their religious, moral, or cultural beliefs. No one should be able to decide for those who wanted to read it that they should not have access to it, he pointed out.

As is often the case with controversial works of art, wherever there was an effort to ban the book, sales in those parts of the country spiked and often skyrocketed. By around 2007, it had sold about eight hundred thousand copies. It has also remained one of the most frequently challenged books on schools' reading lists and at public libraries nationwide, according to the American Library Association (ALA). Every year, the ALA releases a list of the top ten most frequently challenged books, and *Perks* appeared several time during the 2000s.

FROM THE WRITTEN WORD TO THE SILVER SCREEN

The success and influence of *Perks* opened up many doors for Stephen Chbosky. Some first-time novelists do very well transitioning into the world of screenwriting. But Chbosky already had screenwriting experience, and he had already done a great deal in the film industry, even if he had had only limited financial success before his book debuted in 1999.

It was the 1990s, the new era of independent film. He had graduated USC and moved home, and he was determined to make a film on his own terms. He asked friends, family, and acquaintances for money. Like many other beginning independent filmmakers, he applied for credit cards and maxed them out.

A sign welcomes attendees and filmmakers to the 2012 Sundance Film Festival in Park City, Utah. Sundance is one of the largest film festivals in the United States.

In the end, he raised about $50,000. This amount was enough to write, produce, and direct his own movie, *The Four Corners of Nowhere*. Chbosky's film follows the exploits of a hitchhiker named Duncan and all the people he encounters on the way to Ann Arbor, Michigan. It resembles many of the films of the era in that it explores the lives of the creative and philosophical but occasionally aimless members of Generation X, of which Chbosky can be considered a member.

One of the main ways for indie filmmakers to promote and have their films seen—and possibly purchased to be distributed by a major film company—is to have them shown at a prestigious festival. The Sundance Film Festival in Utah, founded in 1978, has helped launch many careers over the years, and it was one of the hottest forums for new talent, especially in the mid-1990s. *The Four Corners of Nowhere* landed a spot at the festival and was later one of the first films to be shown on the festival's new cable outlet, the Sundance Channel. Aside from the prestige of being part of the film festival, it also helped land Chbosky an agent for the first time.

THE MYSTERIES OF PITTSBURGH

One of the most famous literary writers to come out of Chbosky's hometown of Pittsburgh is Michael Chabon, known for *The Amazing Adventures of Kavalier & Clay* and *Wonder Boys*, among other books. *Wonder Boys*, written in 1988, depicts an eccentric college professor who meets an eccentric and talented young student. It overlaps with some themes that Chbosky's novel had explored.

In 2000, Chbosky was ecstatic when he was picked to help write the film version of Chabon's first novel, *The Mysteries of Pittsburgh*. Along with his hometown pride and respect for the more experienced writer's work, it was a perfect project for Chbosky. Chabon's debut was a coming-of-age tale with quirky characters and, like *Perks*, did not shy away from sensitive topics such as homosexuality.

Chbosky wrote the screenplay with John Sherman, and Chabon declared that he was very satisfied with the results. Jason Schwartzman, the star of the coming-of-age comedy *Rushmore*, was set to star in the film. However, the project fell apart unexpectedly just before it looked like filming would actually start.

JOURNEYMAN SCREENWRITER: CHBOSKY DOES *RENT*

Being a fiction writer can be a lonely job, but many writers like it that way. It also mainly involves the creative vision of one person. Editors might suggest or make changes and/or cuts to a manuscript, but out of all the different kinds of professional writers, fiction authors often have the most control over their creative output. While he would one day return to the creative territory he had explored with *Perks* (and to writing a new novel), Chbosky's next move was returning to his first love: the film industry. His success with *Perks* earned him some high-profile attention. Like the high schooler who had enjoyed being involved with musical theater, Chbosky, the sought-after screenwriter, would soon have the chance to be involved with an onscreen adaptation of one of the hottest theater properties of the decade, the film version of the wildly successful musical *Rent*.

Jonathan Larson had written the rock musical *Rent* in the early 1990s, and it first premiered in 1994, moving to Broadway in 1996. Based on Giacomo Puccini's famous opera *La Bohème*, the musical dealt with artists struggling to make it on New York City's Lower East Side in the late 1980s, including gay characters dealing with the life-threatening HIV virus.

Chbosky considered it an honor and a challenge when he was offered the chance to write the screen adaptation of the musical. "Here was an opportunity to write about a group of friends at a certain time in life, dealing with real issues but told through a very hopeful prism," Chbosky told *Written By.*

As with many projects in Hollywood, there were several attempts to produce a film version of *Rent*, and Chbosky ended up attached to two of them. These opportunities gave him valuable experience in collaborating with some premier Hollywood talents.

The first was with acclaimed director Spike Lee, director of *Do the Right Thing*, *X*, *25th Hour*, and many other films. Chbosky worked with Lee during the summer of 2001 to bring the movie to life. "I wrote a draft for Spike and he was really good to me," Chbosky told the *Seattle Post-Intelligencer*. "It's all work for him. He's also a really amazing leader and literally the most intimidating person I've ever met."

Before Chris Columbus took over and completed a film version of *Rent*, Stephen Chbosky had the opportunity to write a version of the screenplay for acclaimed director Spike Lee.

WORKING WITH CHRIS COLUMBUS

Spike Lee's version of *Rent* never went forward, but a few years later, Chris Columbus took over directing duties. Columbus had seen great success with family comedies such as *Home Alone*, *Mrs. Doubtfire*, and the first two film versions of J. K. Rowling's Harry Potter series. Chbosky appreciated his time with Columbus, too, since the director had also started his career by writing screenplays, and he encouraged Chbosky to visit the set to watch the filming. This welcoming approach is in contrast to some directors, who fear that the screenwriter will becoming overly involved, and even bossy, when it comes to how his or her words are being interpreted by a film crew. Chbosky was respectful and hands-off. Learning every step of the way, Chbosky grew confident that he could one day helm a major project.

His film-school training at USC had prepared Chbosky well for an entirely different kind of creative effort from his journey with *Perks*. This experience particularly helped Chbosky nail the technical aspects of filmmaking. He also said it helped him make his amateur mistakes early on and learn from them.

This was also true for the time he spent on his independent film in the years after USC. Looking

Director, producer, and screenwriter Chris Columbus, shown here at the premiere for his film *Rent*, is one of several prominent Hollywood figures with whom Chbosky has collaborated.

back in October 2012 during his interview with DP/30, he said that he was very proud of the work he had done with *The Four Corners of Nowhere.* However, he felt the film was basically a home video compared to some of the productions he would encounter and be a part of later. "[I] came out of film school, made a movie with friends, got it in the can for about $48,000, shot it in Super 16-mm. But we like to joke that half of it is really good, half of it's

WINNING SOME, LOSING SOME

Over time, Chbosky has worked on many different film projects. Some made it to theaters, but most did not. He adapted novelist Alan Brown's book *Audrey Hepburn's Neck*, which was slated to be released by Miramax and directed by Griffin Dunne but ended up not being made. Another film he wrote and was set to be directed by Chbosky himself was *Finger Nails and Smooth Skin*, a romantic comedy. He was even selected to pen a film version of a children's educational cartoon from the 1970s and 1980s, called *Schoolhouse Rock*, before that project, too, was shelved. While they never came to be, each experience helped support Chbosky financially and helped him gain the perspectives and experiences he sought and thrived on. Working with other creative people was a big plus, too.

really not." Of the Sundance Film Festival itself, he said, "It was wonderful to go there, but financially we lost our shirt. Ninety-nine percent of independent movies go nowhere theatrically, which is really tough, so I spent a long time trying to climb out."

When asked whether directing his own film early on had prepared him for his later screenwriting and directorial work, he admitted that it was the collaborative aspects of working with other writers and directors later on in his career that helped him improve his skill set the most. Everyone seemed to have his own way of directing, and the more people Chbosky worked alongside and under, the more confident he grew in his own abilities.

ADAPTING AND ADAPTATION

In *Filmmaker Magazine* in late 2012, Chbosky shared his philosophy on mixing it up creatively with different directors and writers: "The thing I would say to anyone who's aspiring to direct is that if you sit on set, and see the same characters and actors being directed by, say, 12 different people, you realize how much room you have for your own [directing] style. And that gave me a lot of freedom and confidence to realize that I could do it the way that I wanted."

The experience of working with a variety of directors "improved my skills at adapting," Chbosky pointed out to *Written By.* This step forward

Chbosky gives a speech onstage after winning Best First Feature for *The Perks of Being a Wallflower* at the 2013 Independent Spirit Awards, broadcast on February 23 from Santa Monica, California.

developed because he now approached each writing job as "directed" or inspired by the piece itself. Also, as he was not the original creator, he approached his work with more detachment. When it came to adapting *Rent* from the stage to the screen, he had loved the original musical. He knew that plenty of *Rent* fans felt as attached to its characters as his own readers had been to Charlie and his friends. He admitted to *Filmmaker Magazine* that "it took some work to get inside those characters [from *Rent*] . . . but it also gave me some distance and perspective [which made adaptation easier]." *Rent* became a "training ground" and "sparring partner" for his eventual film adaptation of his novel, Chbosky said.

He also told the Examiner.com that writing the adapted screenplay taught him how movies should be inherently objective. In other words, the screenwriter should try to make sure viewers all share a similar experience, even if they may interpret an experience differently. That experience should be the experience of the protagonist. With a novel, he realized, the experience was far more subjective for the reader.

FOUR

CHAPTER

ADVENTURES IN WRITING: TELEVISION AND BEYOND

Stephen Chbosky has always been grateful and eager to try different things. New experiences are exciting in and of themselves, and varying one's ways of writing and creating help to exercise different creative muscles. An author who keeps adding to his or her tool belt, so to speak, is always prepared and is always getting better.

A NEW FRONTIER: TELEVISION AND JERICHO

Television demands some of the same storytelling muscles as film. But it requires different ones than writing prose friction,

Chbosky soon discovered. He had initially been reluctant to make the transition, thinking he would dislike the TV production environment.

In 2004, his agent convinced him to try it out, he told the *Pittsburgh Post-Gazette* in September 2006. "[S]he finally said, 'Listen, I think you have the wrong impression of what TV is about . . .' It turned out she was right. I enjoyed the people in television, the executives, and the producers," he said.

Producer John Turteltaub hired Chbosky for an entirely new idea, a TV show called *Jericho*. Influenced by the ways people coped with real-life disasters such as 9/11 and Hurricane Katrina, the series, which was broadcast by CBS, depicted the aftermath of a nuclear attack that struck twenty-three major cities in the United States. Jericho is a fictional small town in Kansas where the towns-people cope with this crisis.

It was serious subject matter, but according to the website IGN.com, Chbosky joked when he saw the treatment, a short summary of the story: "It's great . . . We could use some girls, a little kissing, and some laughs." Chbosky was instrumental in adding more dramatic and interpersonal elements to the show and in influencing the writers to incorporate more female-centered plotlines.

Chbosky helped create *Jericho* and was hired as a writer and executive producer. He felt part

Actress Ashley Scott is shown here in a scene from the TV series *Jericho*, in which she played a central role as strong-willed and intelligent schoolteacher Emily.

of the reason he was picked was that he was "a character writer who could take a big idea and make it weekly," he told *Written By*. "They had this good premise, and I knew how to create a town because I love writing about communities."

Jericho received positive reviews from critics and attracted devoted fans. Chbosky was touched and flattered by the positive viewer response, which reminded him of *Perks*'s fan response. The show received poor ratings, unfortunately, and ran for only two seasons, from September 2006 until March 2008. There were talks, however, of bringing the series back in the late 2000s. Chbosky even said in February 2013 that producers had discussed the possibility with Netflix, the streaming video and DVD-rental subscription service. Nothing has materialized yet, however. Two comic book companies, Devil's Due Publishing and IDW Publishing, have released comic book series since 2009 that continued the storylines begun on the TV show.

While various directors switched off on directing duties for the show's total of twenty-nine episodes, Chbosky personally wrote "The First Seventeen Hours," the pilot (introductory episode) of the show, which introduced the nuclear attack and its immediate aftermath, as well as the second episode, "Aftermath." Skeet Ulrich, the

JERICHO FANS GO NUTS!

Chbosky's beloved show was actually cancelled not once, but twice. Its low ratings led to its cancellation after the first season. This action led to fan uproar and a motivated, viral campaign to continue the show, which had ended season one on a cliffhanger. Part of the campaign centered on a line spoken by Jake Green, a leading character. During a major conflict, when told to surrender, Green says, "Nuts!," a reference to a general's refusal to give up during World War II's Battle of the Bulge. Referencing this line, fans arranged to have forty thousand pounds of nuts mailed to CBS executives. Another interpretation was that CBS was nuts, or crazy, to cancel their beloved series. Incredibly, the campaign succeeded, and *Jericho* returned for season two.

Skeet Ulrich is shown here as main character Jake Green in a promotional picture for *Jericho*. Fans took to the show enough that the network delayed its cancellation for a time.

actor who played the series' main character, Jake Green, was particularly impressed with the pilot script. He told IGN.com that he thought it was a "story you can't stop thinking about and can't let go," and was hooked on his character's complicated background. He was most intrigued by the premise and how the script explored the way the situation changed the characters.

TV'S TAKEAWAYS

One skill that Chbosky gained from writing for television was the ability to tell a story in an immediate manner. The events onscreen during an episode of television have to give the viewer lots of information in much less time than in a novel or film. "When you write a pilot, you have 40 minutes to introduce [in the case of *Jericho*] 21 characters," he told *Filmmaker Magazine.* This taught Chbosky how to edit quickly and chop off unnecessary pieces of story that did not push a plot forward. TV "strives to be incredibly clear," Chbosky noted in *Written By.*

Seeing how much was cut from an original script and how different it was from what eventually showed up onscreen every week was a learning experience, too. Actually, it was liberating for Chbosky. It taught him not to get too attached to what he was writing. Novelists have license to wander, create moods, and explore their characters' minds. TV writers do not have this luxury because viewers are not likely to tune in again if things move too slowly. The scriptwriter must be flexible and adjust to the needs of the plot, the pace, and the audience, unlike a novelist, who relies on his or her own vision.

OPENING DOORS

Besides developing new creative powers, his TV work gave Chbosky some degree of financial freedom. The money was important because for many years, Hollywood players had approached the author with offers for the film rights to *Perks*. Had he not been as successful, it would have been more painful to refuse the big cash payout for his most cherished creative effort.

Chbosky had also seen firsthand a sad fact of life when it came to screenwriting and moviemaking: even some fantastic scripts never get made. The right balance of financial backing, writing, casting, and directing must be achieved before a decent piece of filmmaking can be made, much less one that is entertaining and resonates with audiences.

Screenplays or ideas that start out well but end up nowhere are known in the film industry as being in "development hell." Sometimes, too many people attempt to contribute their creative input, and the original vision of the screenwriter, or the idea itself, is lost. Chbosky owed a debt to himself to tell the story a second time, the right way. But he also felt *Perks*'s fans deserved the best.

It was never really an option to give up control of *Perks*; he would never be happy unless he wrote and directed his own film. "I was either going to make this movie or it wasn't going to exist. I could never give it away," he told *Filmmaker Magazine*. Even when he had gone through hard times and the offers were there, he knew he would always regret it if he gave in and allowed others to control, change, and possibly ruin his vision for what the movie could be.

JACK-OF-ALL-TRADES

Everything that Chbosky has done has informed his creative process and helped him grow as an artist. Even minor projects can be rewarding, and Chbosky has gained a reputation as a jack-of-all-trades, someone who can do it all. Not long after *Perks* became an audience sensation, Chbosky's newfound fame earned him a gig editing a fiction anthology, or collection of stories, by a group of up-and-coming young writers. Because he had con-nected so powerfully with so many young readers, the author was deemed a natural candidate to edit the collection.

In addition to its television programming, MTV Networks has launched several media enterprises over time, including MTV Books, which published a fiction anthology with which Chbosky became involved.

Published in August 2000, *Pieces: A Collection of New Voices* was released by Chbosky's own publisher, MTV Books. The stories compiled in *Pieces* were picked from submissions to MTV's Write Stuff

competition. Chbosky not only edited the volume
but also wrote the introduction. In it, he relates the
tale of how he got the news that *Perks* was to be
published and how it felt when he saw his book in
the bookstore for the first time.

He made the point that each person—the writer,
the reader, the publishers, and others—are all part of
the community that makes books and makes literary
movements happen. "As difficult and breakneck as
our society can be at times, it is my belief that we
can have that community, and all it takes is someone creating something, someone else being willing
to put it out there, and someone else being willing to
look at it for what it is," Chbosky wrote.

KEPT: A BOOK OF A MUSICAL

Before he tried his hand at a cinematic adaptation of *Rent*, Chbosky collaborated with lyricist and
singer Bill Russell and composer Henry Krieger to
write the script of the two producers' coproduction,
Kept. *Kept* was a musical, with the performance
debuting in 2002 for a limited run at TheatreWorks
in Mountain View, California. Chbosky gained the
experience of adapting one creative format into
another—in this case, from a live production into
a book, a direction many writers do not get the
chance to tackle.

VERSATILITY, INSPIRATION, AND ADVICE

An interviewer for the Phoenix Film Festival in 2012 asked Chbosky which creative activity he favored: writing or directing. He answered that he loved writing novels and film directing the best. They gave him the most joy. While screenwriting satisfied him, it was much tougher work. "That's where you pay all your dues," he told the interviewer. The most difficult part was the technicality of the work itself. He quoted Ted Tally, the writer of the Best Picture–winning horror/thriller *The Silence of the Lambs*, who described adaptation as "turning soup back into bullion."

This joy was most easily found by "writing what you know," he observed. Chbosky had brought Charlie and his friends to life by drawing from the emotional memories of his own teen years. However, he added, "Maybe it's about going one step further and write what you love? Write with your honest emotion." With screenwriting, there was less room for truth, emotion, and expression because it was a necessary and occasionally tough job the screenwriter had to do.

For Chbosky, there is no specific technical advice he has to offer other writers or other creative

Screenwriter Stewart Stern is shown here at the Rome Film Festival in October 2011. Chbosky credits Stern and other encouraging mentors with helping him find his voice and inspiring him in his creative work.

people. Instead, he has taken to heart the encouragement he received from Stewart Stern regarding any creative work, or anything in life, for that matter. "So many of us, for whatever reason, believe that we can't do it, believe we can't achieve it, or even worse, believe that we don't deserve it, even if we work really hard for it," he said.

"Pay attention, nurture, support, challenge, and find that voice that is uniquely yours, the passion that is uniquely yours, it will lead you to your best work," Chbosky told the *Daily Trojan*. "Do it for those personal reasons because that's going to lead to the most authentic story and the most authentic personal story ironically becomes the most universal."

Chbosky did his best to follow his own advice when he finally undertook his most challenging project ever: taking his most personal work and transforming it into a film that would feel emotionally honest to audiences, while working in the entirely different format of cinema. The essential truths should remain the same, no matter the medium.

FULL-CIRCLE, FULL-STEAM AHEAD: THE PERKS OF BEING A DIRECTOR

The skills Chbosky had honed from his film-school days through his breakthrough success to his television era all seemed to be preparation for his most ambitious and difficult task yet: bringing *The Perks of Being a Wallflower* to the silver screen. He told the DP/30 vlog, "I could not possibly have directed this movie before I went through those experiences, because . . . it was such a difficult screenplay to write."

There were many challenges in getting the project off the ground, both technical and emotional. He had to handle several roles at once, approaching the material both as the original novelist, a screenwriter, and as the director. This film would surely test all his creative resources— sometimes all of them simultaneously it seemed! But he had been awaiting this opportunity for more than ten years.

NOVEL VS. SCREENPLAY

One of the first challenges was in adapting the screenplay itself. With another book, Chbosky would have already had a certain amount of distance and objectivity in relation to the material. Adapting *Perks* was far trickier. He applied some lessons from TV: show a lot and do not be afraid to cut anything that takes away from the bare story you are telling. "There's a difference between filming a script and making a movie," as Chbosky told Vulture.com.

A major obstacle was that this first-person epis- tolary novel would have to be transformed into a third-person narrative screenplay and then filmed. It was two whole steps removed from the source and an entirely different perspective. Considering this new approach, he told the Examiner.com, he took a "kitchen-sink" approach, by including everything in the book into a very long first draft. He knew the value of distance and took a few months' break from writing the screenplay.

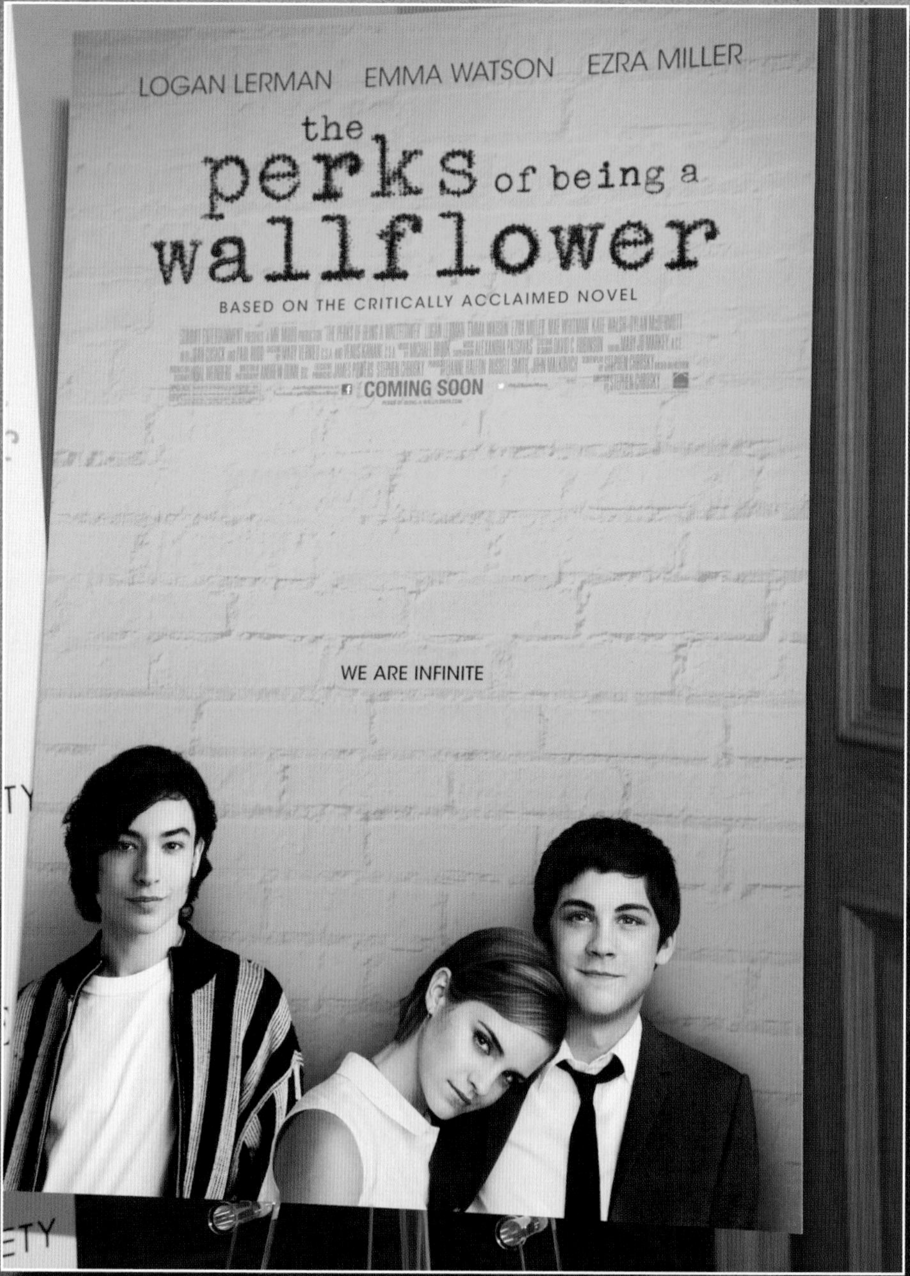

The poster for the film version of *The Perks of Being a Wallflower* is shown here. Chbosky was particularly pleased with the performances of Ezra Miller, Emma Watson, and Logan Lerman *(seen here left to right)*, who played the teenaged leads.

Chbosky returned to the script, making it lean and mean: the old "When in doubt, leave it out" method. It also read differently because of the time off he had taken, having become more like someone else's work. He could now be more objective. He consciously excluded everything that did not deal with Charlie and his friends' actions.

TOUGH CHALLENGES

Chbosky revealed to Vulture.com that perhaps the hardest scene in the film was one where a pivotal character breaks down emotionally. Writing on paper that a character cries gives a lone reader all he or she needs to know. To convey the same action onscreen requires that the actor cast in the scene is believable. The emotional impact of the scene has to connect but not overdo it for the viewer.

In addition, there is an "aha" moment in the book that is moved to a place earlier in the film's narrative. To provide a climax later on that the audience finds satisfying, Chbosky combined footage of a character at two different times in his life existing in the same scene, or space. When he saw the footage side by side, he knew he had his new "aha" moment.

Chbosky also had certain ideas of how scenes from the book would play onscreen. However, he remained flexible, trusting his instincts. If something else captured on film fit the mood and story better, he ran with it. "I had it in my mind that after they graduated, the characters would run up this hill," he told Vulture.com, "and there was a hill that I'd always wanted to film. I'm talking seventeen years that I wanted to film this shot." While filming, the crew captured a beautiful picture of the bleachers at sunset, and Chbosky suddenly decided that this was the image to use, instead of the hill.

Chbosky discovered while filming *Perks* that one could do things on the screen that would not work on the page. Creative editing can move the story forward while showing the passage of time effectively and be entertaining in the process. "The one thing that movies have is editing, it's juxtaposition," Chbosky told the *Daily Trojan.* "In a book you can never have a kid taking a communion at Christmas, and cut from him taking the communion wafer to his mouth and taking his hand away, and now we're inside a New Year's Eve party. I love it."

THE PERKS OF FILMING

Other elements of the production that excited Chbosky were the filming locations and the onscreen and off-screen talent teaming up to make the movie. Chbosky and his casting directors selected some up-and-coming young actors, including Logan Lerman as Charlie and Ezra Miller

Chbosky *(left)* directs Emma Watson *(second from right)* and Logan Lerman *(right)* on set in 2012. Filming his own novel challenged the writer, forcing him to hone his creative powers.

as Patrick. Emma Watson, who played Sam, was especially famous among younger viewers for her career playing Hermione from the Harry Potter film franchise. Chbosky personally approved most of the main cast and auditioned about 450 young people for the teenage roles.

Chbosky revealed to Alexandra Dresch of the online high school newspaper *Blueprint* his partial motivation in casting someone very charismatic

in the role of Patrick. "[W]hen I was making *Perks* the movie, I wanted Ferris Bueller to be the gay kid. Because he never is, you know? And I wanted him to be the most fearless, most confident, funniest, coolest, over-it and the most profound non-victim you've ever met."

A CRACK PRODUCTION TEAM

Chbosky was also happy to have a production team that had been responsible for some of his favorite films of the last twenty years. Mr. Mudd productions included producers Lianne Halfon, Russ Smith, and actor, director, and producer John Malkovich. Mr. Mudd had done a few critically acclaimed coming-of-age films, too, including *Ghost World*, featuring one of Scarlett Johansson's earlier

John Malkovich is shown at the photo shoot of his play *Les Liaisons Dangereuses (Dangerous Liaisons)*, a stage version of the novel by the same name. Malkovich starred in a screen version of this story in the 1980s.

performances, and *Juno*, starring Ellen Page. The director even told the *Seattle Post-Intelligencer* how John Malkovich gave him a pep talk during filming, playing on Chbosky's hometown pride. "I love your script because it has heart," Chbosky quoted. "You have heart and you don't need sentiment. Direct this movie like a guy from Pittsburgh and always get the tough take."

STARRING . . . PITTSBURGH

Another character in the story, and nearly as important to Chbosky as the living actors themselves, was the director's own hometown. Much of it was filmed in and around Pittsburgh and in Peters Township in Washington County, Pennsylvania, which borders Chbosky's home of Upper St. Clair. It added so much to the production for Chbosky to set this very personal story in places that had meant so much to him growing up.

One famous set piece from the book, which was among the very first ideas he came up with for the novel, was a scene where a character rides standing up in the back of a moving pickup truck through a tunnel. In the film, Emma Watson's

Emma Watson rides in the back of a pickup truck during one of the pivotal scenes of the *Perks* film, an iconic moment in the movie and a nod to fellow Pittsburghers.

Sam rides with her arms outstretched through Pittsburgh's Fort Pitt Tunnel. For Chbosky, it would not have quite been the same to film in a random tunnel in some other unfamiliar city.

PERKS AND EXTRAS: A FAMILY AFFAIR

Chbosky took advantage of shooting in Pittsburgh to include some very personal touches. A scene where Charlie's Aunt Helen speaks to him was filmed on Chbosky's own childhood street, with his family's home within a stone's throw of the film crew. Chbosky recounted a funny moment about pairing his real-life family with Charlie's screen family together while filming a communion scene. With their local Bethel Presbyterian Church disguised as a Catholic one, Lea and Fred Chbosky sat with actors Kate Walsh and Dylan McDermott. Fred Chbosky was at the very end of only one shot, while his mother received more screen time. Chbosky was more than happy to use their property for filming, too, since it earned his retiree parents a location fee. His sister, Stacy, also played a young mother in the film.

GOING FULL-CIRCLE

Chbosky considers the film version to be the greatest artistic and creative experience of his entire life. It might be because of—and not in spite of—the fact that it was a longer and more difficult process than writing the book itself. The novel spilled out of him almost effortlessly, he has often pointed out. The movie required a great deal of thought and care, especially when it came to isolating the personal truths and influences from the novel and presenting them in a way that would still ring true onscreen.

The Perks of Being a Wallflower seemed to hit all the right notes with film audiences. Chbosky attributed part of its success to its dual nature. He believed that he had filmed a story that appealed both to the urgency of teens growing up with enough appeal for an older adult audience's sense of nostalgia. The early 1990s setting and sound track did not hurt with the latter sector. In addition, many diehard fans of the book felt it was a true and faithful version of their beloved book. For many young filmgoers, it became an instant classic, like its source material.

Critics were impressed, too. News outlets mostly praised the young actors and some of the supporting adult roles, too, such as Paul Rudd's portrayal of Charlie's English teacher, Mr. Anderson. The film,

Chbosky's screenplay, and the performances garnered awards from many cities' film critics' circles and societies, including Boston, Phoenix, Detroit, and others. In 2013, *Perks* received many honors as a standout production for 2012. The Writers Guild of America nominated Chbosky's script for Best Adapted Screenplay, the MTV Movie Awards nominated Emma Watson and Ezra Miller for their acting, and Logan Lerman, Watson, and the film itself all won Teen Choice Awards that year.

When the film premiered in Seattle in late 2012, Chbosky was able to live

Logan Lerman is shown onstage accepting the Teen Choice Award for his performance in *Perks*, at the Gibson Amphitheatre in Universal City, California, August 11, 2013.

out one of his lifelong dreams. Following the premiere, he was joined at a question-and-answer (Q&A) session by his longtime teacher and friend, Stewart Stern. "It was one of the greatest moments of my life, to finally sit side by side with the greatest teacher I ever had and talk about our work," Chbosky said. "It was definitely an infinite moment for me," he added, referencing a famous line from the film that signified the characters' search for meaning in life.

FAMILY MAN

The film's triumph, the greatest of a set of growing successes over the past decade since the debut of his novel, has been one of several infinite moments for Chbosky. Much of this drive and willingness to embrace life flowed from his earlier success with *Perks* the novel. "The book has changed my life in every way it could have. Because of my book, I met my wife Liz, I got my first job in television, and I made the movie, which was the culmination of a 21-year dream," he told World Book Night.

Chbosky and his wife Liz (née Maccie) were engaged in 2010 and later married that same year on September 18, at the Inn of the Seventh Ray in Malibu, California. The following year, Chbosky directed *Perks*, and he also found out that he was going to be the father of a baby girl. In 2012, the

Chbosky and his wife, Liz, smile for the cameras at the *Perks* premiere at the Cinerama Dome in Los Angeles, California, September 10, 2012.

year *Perks* was released in theaters, his daughter was born. Maccie Margaret Chbosky was given his wife's maiden name as her first name in honor of his father-in-law. A couple of weeks after her birth, he wrote how he hoped that, in fifteen years, his teenage daughter would gain comfort from his work during whatever growing pains she might experience.

BACK TO WORK

The future should continue to prove busy for Stephen Chbosky. One possible idea has Chbosky teaming up with his wife in a creative partnership so that they might adapt other young adult (YA) novels for the screen. (Chbosky's wife, Liz Maccie, is a screenwriter and actress in her own right, who has written episodes of the ABC Family broadcast show *Make It or Break It*.)

Many fans have wondered for years if Chbosky would ever get back to novel writing. They may not have to wait much longer. In May 2013, the writer told the *Pittsburgh Post-Gazette* that he was finally embarking on a new fiction project. This time he would go back even further than the 1990s, setting his new story in the 1970s. "It has very similar themes and emotions as 'Perks,'" he told the *Gazette*, "but it's done almost as a vintage novel from Stephen King in the 1970s." The setting for this still-unnamed project would once again be western Pennsylvania, and Chbosky hints that he may even incorporate some element of the supernatural.

Whatever creative road Chbosky travels down—and whatever kind of writing he undertakes—it is likely he will continue to win new fans and to connect with readers and viewers on a very deep emotional level. For his ever-growing fan base out there, that will be definitely be one of the perks of being an avid reader of Stephen Chbosky.

ON STEPHEN CHBOSKY

Name: Stephen Chbosky
Birth date: January 25, 1970
Birthplace: Pittsburgh, Pennsylvania
Current residence: Los Angeles, California
First creative work (film): *The Four Corners of Nowhere*, 1995
First publication: *The Perks of Being a Wallflower*, 1999
Marital status: Married
Spouse: Liz Maccie Chbosky
Children: Maccie Margaret Chbosky (b. 2012)
Siblings: Stacy Chbosky, actress and director (b. 1972)
Education: Streams Elementary School, Pittsburgh, Pennsylvania; Upper St. Clair High School, Pittsburgh, Pennsylvania, 1988; University of Southern California (USC), Los Angeles, California, School of Cinematic Arts, master of fine arts (MFA) in writing, 1992
Major awards:

American Library Association (ALA) Best Books for Young Adults Award, 2000, for *The Perks of Being a Wallflower*

Chlotrudis Award [Chlotrudis Society for Independent Film], Best Adapted Screenplay for *The Perks of Being a Wallflower*, 2013

Independent Spirit Award, Best First Feature for *The Perks of Being a Wallflower*, 2013

ON STEPHEN CHBOSKY'S WORK

The Four Corners of Nowhere 1995 (film) (writer/director)

Hitchhiker and nomad Duncan hitches a ride with performance artist Toad on the way to Ann Arbor, Michigan, where they fall in with Toad's sister, her law student fiancé, and an assortment of other colorful slacker characters.

Premiered: Sundance Film Festival, 1995

Award: Best Narrative Feature, Chicago Underground Film Festival

The Perks of Being a Wallflower MTV Books/Pocket Books, 1999

This movie is about a year in the life of a detached yet talented and sensitive introvert going through a tumultuous and exciting freshman year of high school in a suburb of Pittsburgh. The novel takes the form of a series of letters to a stranger, in which Charlie copes with death, deals with social alienation, and tries his hand at real friendship and romance.

Published: February 1, 1999
Awards: Bluegrass Award; Garden State Teen Book Award; Volunteer State Book Award

Rent (screenplay), 2005, (Dir. Chris Columbus)
Rent is the film version of the breakthrough rock musical of the same name, which stars an ensemble cast playing struggling bohemian artists coping with the ups and downs and tragedies of life on New York's Lower East Side at the end of the 1980s.
Released: November 23, 2005

Jericho (writer/executive producer), September 2006–March 25, 2008 (CBS)
Chbosky helped create this post-apocalyptic vision of what happens to the residents of a fictional Kansas town after modern civilization collapses in the United States after a series of nuclear attacks. Former survivalist Jake Green helps the other town members through their struggles and conflicts, while dealing with the shadows of his own past.
Premiered: September 20, 2006

The Perks of Being a Wallflower film (adapted screenplay; director)
Based on his own best-selling coming-of-age novel, Stephen Chbosky depicts the poignant onscreen

highs and lows of Charlie, a sensitive and with-drawn suburban teenager dealing with love, loss, friendship, and self-acceptance. Set in early 1990s Pittsburgh, the film stars Logan Lerman, Emma Watson, and Ezra Miller.

Released: September 8, 2012 (Toronto International Film Festival)

Awards: GLAAD Media Award for Outstanding Film (2013); People's Choice Awards: Favorite Drama (2013); Teen Choice Awards: Drama (2013).

The Perks of Being a Wallflower (novel, 1999)

"Aspiring filmmaker/first-novelist Chbosky adds an upbeat ending to a tale of teenaged angst—the right combination of realism and uplift to allow it on high school reading lists . . . Charlie oozes sincerity, rails against celebrity phoniness, and feels an extraliterary bond with his favorite writers. A plain-written narrative suggesting that passivity, and thinking too much, lead to confusion and anxiety." —*Kirkus Reviews, February 4, 1999*

"Presented as a series of letters from Charlie to an anonymous friend, this book goes back 10 years to a boy in the midst of a group of friends desperately trying to hide the fact that they are lost. *Perks* is not overly shocking, but it lays in front of the reader something sad, yet somewhat hopeful, and by the end, very satisfying." —Rod Machen, *Austin Chronicle*, October 15, 1999

"Chbosky has a vivid writing style. He is able to capture so many things with a select few words. This is just one of the reasons why I fell in love with this compelling tale. It taught me to see things from a different perspective, just one of the perks of this truly amazing book." —Esther T., Teenink.com

The Perks of Being a Wallflower (film, 2012)

"The movie confirms one of my convictions: If you are too popular in high school, you may become so fond of the feeling that you never find out who you really are. The film is based on Stephen Chbosky's best-selling young-adult novel, which was published in 1999 and is now on many shelves next to *The Catcher in the Rye.* It offers the rare pleasure of an author directing his own book, and doing it well. No one who loves the book will complain about the movie, and especially not about its near-ideal casting." —Roger Ebert, September 26, 2012

". . . Miraculously, though, he's managed to turn his powerful written words into a powerful movie, which opens in limited release today. How'd he do it? By respecting his book's storytelling conceit without being confined by it, by embracing film's unique ability to evoke emotions, and by enlisting a pitch-perfect crew of actors. It's a recipe that other authors-turned-directors-of-their-own-work would be wise to follow." —Ian Buckwalter, *Atlantic,* September 21, 2012

1970 Stephen Chbosky is born on January 25, in Pittsburgh, Pennsylvania.

1988 Chbosky graduates Upper St. Clair High School.

1992 He completes his MFA in writing at USC School of Cinematic Arts.

1994 The first lines of his first novel come to him.

1995 Chbosky writes, directs, and coproduces an indie film, *The Four Corners of Nowhere*, which plays at the Sundance Film Festival.

1999 *The Perks of Being a Wallflower* is published on February 1.

2000 Chbosky edits *Pieces*, a literary anthology of up-and-coming young writers.

2005 The film version of *Rent* is released on November 23.

2006 *Jericho* premieres on September 20.

2010 Chbosky marries Liz Maccie on September 18.

2012 Maccie Margaret Chbosky, the author's daughter, is born in August. Directed and written by Chbosky, the film version of *The Perks of Being a Wallflower* is released at the Toronto International Film Festival (TIFF) on September 8.

ALIENATION Feeling separate or apart from others, such as friends, family, or one's community.

ASPIRING Wanting to be something, such as a writer or filmmaker.

AVID Passionate or dedicated to something.

CATHARSIS The emotional release a reader gets from an intense event in a story.

COLLABORATIVE Dealing with collaboration, or working together to achieve something.

CONVEY To communicate to someone.

CRITICALLY ACCLAIMED Ranked highly or praised by critics.

EPISTOLARY A written work that forms from a series of letters.

EPONYMOUS Describes a person giving his or her name to something; for example, an album named after the musician who creates it.

FLOURISH Grow or develop in a healthy way.

GENERATION X A term describing the generation of Americans born between the early 1960s through the 1970s.

INDIE Describes art—mostly music and film—made without the financial help of big record companies or film studios.

INNOVATIVE Trying new things in one's art, technology, or other disciplines.

INTANGIBLE Unable to be touched; not having a physical presence, but instead a psychological or spiritual one.

INTERPERSONAL Dealing with issues between and among people.

IN THE CAN Film industry term for completing a movie.

JACK-OF-ALL-TRADES A person who can do many different things well.

JUXTAPOSITION The effect of seeing two things near or next to each other.

MENTOR A person who teaches a younger or less experienced person a craft or skill.

NARRATIVE A story, whether a book, short story, television show, or film.

NÉE From the French for "born as," refers to a person's name at birth.

NOSTALGIA A pleasure or sadness (sometimes both) that arises when someone thinks about the past.

NOTORIETY Being famous or well known for doing something bad or negative.

PILOT The first and introductory episode of a television series.

POST-APOCALYPTIC Describing the situation and environment following a disaster of far-reaching proportions.

PREP SCHOOL Short for preparatory school, a private high school that prepares young people for college.

PRESTIGIOUS Well regarded or well thought of in its field.

PROTAGONIST The main character of a narrative.

Q&A Stands for question-and-answer session.

QUIRKY Describes someone who is unusual, original, or eccentric.

SET PIECE A scene in a film that is carefully composed or planned.

SMORGASBORD A large mixture of many different things, named after the Scandinavian word for a serving table with a great variety of foods.

SPARRING PARTNER A person with whom a boxer or other fighter trains.

THIRD PERSON A narrative style in which the characters are described objectively as he, she, it, they, or similar terms.

UNDERDOG In a competition, the person less or least expected to win.

UNREQUITED Refers to attention or love that is not given back in return.

VLOGGER A person who runs or produces a video blog, or "vlog."

WALLFLOWER A loner or person who likes to remain in the background and is afraid of social interaction.

American Screenwriters Association (ASA)
118 William Howard Taft Road
Cincinnati, OH 45219
(513) 221-7014
Website: http://www.americanscreenwriters.com
The American Screenwriters Association is a nonprofit,
    professional association organized for the educa-
    tion, promotion, and encouragement of the art and
    craft of screenwriting.

Canadian Society of Children's Authors, Illustrators
    and Performers (CANSCAIP)
720 Bathurst Street, Suite 504,
Toronto, ON M5S 2R4
Canada
(416) 515-1559
E-mail: office@canscaip.org
Website: http://www.canscaip.org
CANSCAIP supports and promotes children's litera-
    ture and its practitioners through print, media, and
    online efforts, as well as meetings and conferences.

Maurice Kanbar Institute of Film and Television
New York University (NYU)/Tisch School of the Arts
721 Broadway
New York, NY 10003
(212) 998-1800
Website: http://about.tisch.nyu.edu
The Maurice Kanbar Institute, part of NYU's Tisch

School of the Arts, is one of the most prestigious
film schools in the United States.

New York Film Academy (NYFA)
100 East 17th Street
New York, NY 10003
(212) 674-4300
(800) 611-3456
E-mail: film@nyfa.edu
Website: http://www.nyfa.edu
The New York Film Academy is an acting and filmmaking school based in New York City that bills itself as
having the "most hands-on intensive programs in
the world."

Pocket Books
1230 Avenue of the Americas
New York, NY 10020
(212) 698-7000
Website: http://www.simonandschuster.com
Pocket Books, a division of Simon & Schuster, is the
publishing company that put out *The Perks of
Being a Wallflower* via its MTV Books imprint.

School of Cinematic Arts
University of Southern California (USC)
930 W. 34th Street SCB-105
Los Angeles, CA 90089-2211
(213) 740-8358

E-mail: admissions@cinema.usc.edu

Website: https://cinema.usc.edu

Stephen Chbosky's alma mater, the University of
Southern California's (USC) School of Cinematic
Arts, is one of the top film schools in the United
States.

Society of Children's Book Writers and Illustrators
(SCBWI)

8271 Beverly Boulevard

Los Angeles, CA 90048

(323) 782-1892

Website: http://www.scbwi.org

The Society of Children's Book Writers and
Illustrators is an international professional organization comprised of individuals writing and
illustrating specifically for young adult and child
audiences. It welcomes those involved in children's literature, magazines, film, and multimedia.

Sundance Institute

5900 Wilshire Boulevard Suite 800

Los Angeles, CA 90036

(310) 360-1981

E-mail: institute@sundance.org

Website: http://www.sundance.org

The Sundance Institute promotes independent
filmmaking and runs the most well-known

independent film festival in the United States, the Sundance Film Festival.

Writers Guild of America, West (WGA)
7000 W. 3rd Street
Los Angeles, CA 90048
(323) 951-4000
Website: http://www.wga.org
The WGA is a trade union representing writers in the motion picture, broadcast, cable, and new media industries. For certain jobs in these industries, you must be a member of the WGA. For those writers on the East Coast, there also exists the Writers Guild of America, East.

Writers Guild of Canada (WGC)
366 Adelaide Street W., Suite 401
Toronto, ON M5V 1R9
Canada
(416) 979-7907
(800) 567-9974
E-mail: info@wgc.ca
Website: http://www.wgc.ca/contact.html
The Writers Guild of Canada is a professional organization representing the interests and education of more than 2,100 English-language Canadian screenwriters.

The Writers Studio
78 Charles Street, #3R
New York, NY 10014
(212) 255-7075
Website: http://www.writerstudio.com
The Writers Studio welcomes beginning and experienced fiction writers and poets for writing workshops, offering classes in New York; Tucson, Arizona; Amsterdam, Netherlands; and also online, via classes and one-on-one Skype or phone sessions.

Young Adult Library Services Association (YALSA)/
American Library Association (ALA)
50 East Huron Street
Chicago, IL 60611
(800) 545-2433
Website: http://www.ala.org/yalsa
The Young Adult Library Services Association works to strengthen and expand library services for readers ages twelve to eighteen.

WEBSITES

Because of the changing nature of Internet links, Rosen Publishing has developed an online list of websites related to the subject of this book. This site is updated regularly. Please use this link to access this list:

http://www.rosenlinks.com/AAA/Chbo

Chbosky, Stephen. *The Perks of Being a Wallflower.* New York, NY: MTV Books/Simon & Schuster, 2012 (Reprint).

Chbosky, Stephen, ed. *Pieces.* New York, NY: MTV Books/Simon & Schuster, 2012 (Reprint).

Christie, Thomas A. *John Hughes and Eighties Cinema.* Kent, England: Crescent Moon Publishing, 2009.

Elish, Dan. *Plays* (Craft of Writing). New York, NY: Cavendish Square Publishing, 2011.

Elish, Dan. *Screenplays* (Craft of Writing). New York, NY: Cavendish Square Publishing, 2011.

Ferguson. *Writing* (Careers in Focus). New York, NY: Chelsea House, 2007.

Hagler, Gina. *Sarah Dessen* (All About the Author). New York, NY: Rosen Publishing, 2014.

Halverson, Deborah. *Writing Young Adult Fiction for Dummies.* Hoboken, NJ: For Dummies/Wiley Publishing, 2011.

Hamilton, John. *Screenplay* (You Write It!). Mankato, MN: Abdo Publishing, 2009.

Jenks, Andrew. *Andrew Jenks: My Adventures as a Young Filmmaker.* New York, NY: Scholastic Press, 2013.

Knowles, John. *A Separate Peace.* New York, NY: Scribner, 2014 (Reprint).

Manser, Martin H. *The Facts On File Guide to Good Writing.* New York, NY: Chelsea House, 2005.

Mara, Wil. *Steven Spielberg* (Great Filmmakers). New York, NY: Cavendish Square Publishing, 2014.

Potter, Ellen, and Anne Mazer. *Spilling Ink: A Young Writer's Handbook.* New York, NY: Square Fish Books, 2010.

Salinger, J. D. *The Catcher in the Rye.* New York, NY: Little, Brown and Company, 1991.

Segall, Miriam. *Career Building Through Fan Fiction.* New York, NY: Rosen Publishing, 2008.

Skog, Jason. *Screenwriting: A Practical Guide to Pursuing the Art* (The Performing Arts). Mankato, MN: Capstone Press, 2010.

Staley, Erin. *Maggie Stiefvater* (All About the Author). New York, NY: Rosen Publishing, 2014.

Wolny, Philip. *James Dashner* (All About the Author). New York, NY: Rosen Publishing, 2014.

Airdo, Joseph. "Author Stephen Chbosky Realizes Dreams with 'Perks of Being a Wallflower' Film." Examiner.com, September 27, 2012. Retrieved March 20, 2014 (http://www.examiner.com/article/author-stephen-chbosky-realizes-dreams-with-perks-of-being-a-wallflower-film).

Aquino, Tara. "Interview: 'The Perks of Being a Wallflower' Director Stephen Chbosky Talks Finding the Perfect Cast and Changing Teens' Lives." Complex.com, September 22, 2012. Retrieved March 27, 2014 (http://www.complex.com/pop-culture/2012/09/interview-the-perks-of-being-a-wallflower-director-stephen-chbosky).

Brindle, Becky. "Hollywood Director 'Proud to Come Home' to Upper St. Clair." *Upper St. Clair Patch*, September 30, 2013. Retrieved March 29, 2014 (http://upperstclair.patch.com/groups/schools/p/hollywood-director-proud-to-come-home-to-upper-st-clair).

Buchanan, Kyle. "The Toughest Scene I Wrote: Perks of Being a Wallflower Writer-Director Stephen Chbosky." Vulture.com, January 2, 2013. Retrieved April 7, 2014 (http://www.vulture.com/2012/12/toughest-scene-perks-of-being-a-wallflower.html).

Chbosky, Stephen, ed. *Pieces*. New York, NY: MTV Books/Simon & Schuster, 2012 (Reprint).

Dersch, Alexandra. "Interview with Perks of Being a Wallflower's Stephen Chbosky." *Blueprint*

Magazine, September 2012. Retrieved April 10, 2014 (http://blueprintonline.blogspot.com/2012/09/interview-with-perks-of-being.html).

"DP/30: The Perks of Being a Wallflower, Writer/Director Stephen Chbosky, Actor Ezra Miller." September 20, 2012. Retrieved March 28, 2014 (https://www.youtube.com/watch?v=rxnN8thYzEQ).

Durling, Roger. "The Perks of Being a Wallflower Q&A." Santa Barbara International Film Festival, September 26, 2012. Retrieved March 28, 2014 (http://sbiff.org/wallflower-qa).

Fetters, Sara Michelle. "'The Perks of Being a Wallflower'—Interview with Author/Screenwriter/Director Stephen Chbosky." Moviefreak.com, September 21, 2012. Retrieved April 5, 2014 (http://www.moviefreak.com/artman/publish/interviews_perkswallflower_stephenchbosky.shtml).

Goldman, Eric. "Paley Fest: Jericho." IGN.com, March 15, 2007. Retrieved April 7, 2014 (http://www.ign.com/articles/2007/03/15/paley-fest-jericho).

Hall, Tim. "Q&A with Writer/Director Stephen Chbosky." *Seattle Post-Intelligencer*, September 23, 2012. Retrieved April 2, 2014 (http://blog.seattlepi.com/peoplescritic/2012/09/23/qa-with-writerdirector-stephen-chbosky).

Handy, Bruce. "Q&A: Perks of Being a Wallflower's Stephen Chbosky on Emma Watson's Casting,

High School Yearning, and 'Heroes.'" *Vanity Fair*, October 5, 2012. Retrieved April 5, 2014 (http://www.vanityfair.com/online/oscars/2012/10/qa -stephen-chbosky-perks-of-being-a-wallflower).

Hanlon, John. "Stephen Chbosky." John Hanlon Reviews, September 27, 2012. Retrieved March 28, 2014 (http://www.johnhanlonreviews.com/ interview/stephen-chbosky-interview).

Krochmal, Shana Naomi. "Stephen Chbosky Explains Why 'Perks' Had to Be PG-13." *Out*, September 18, 2012. Retrieved April 1, 2014 , (http://www.out.com/entertainment/movies/2012/ 09/18/stephen-chbosky-perks-being-wallflower).

Mansky, Jacqueline. "Perks Creator Credits Versatility to USC." *Daily Trojan*, October 2, 2012. Retrieved March 2, 2014 (http:// dailytrojan.com/2012/10/02/perks-creator -credits-versatility-to-usc).

Marra, Andy. "GLSEN Chats with Author and Film Director Stephen Chbosky." Gay, Lesbian & Straight Education Network, May 3, 2013. Retrieved April 12, 2014 (http://blog.glsen.org/ blog/glsen-chats-author-and-film-director -stephen-chbosky).

Maughan, Shannon. "MTV Lands 'The List' by Siobhan Vivian." *Publishers Weekly*, December 13, 2013. Retrieved March 29, 2014 (http://www.publishersweekly.com/pw/

by-topic/childrens/childrens-book-news/
article/60378-mtv-lands-the-list-by-siobhan
-vivian.html).

Osenlund, R. Kurt. "Writer/Director Stephen
Chbosky on *The Perks of Being a Wallflower.*"
Filmmaker Magazine, September 21, 2012 (http://
filmmakermagazine.com/52492-writerdirector
-stephen-chbosky-on-the-perks-of-being-a
-wallflower/#.U0tXbFwru1A).

Owen, Rob. "Upper St. Clair Graduate Writes for
CBS's 'Jericho.'" *Pittsburgh Post-Gazette*,
September 10, 2006. Retrieved March 2, 2014
(http://www.post-gazette.com/ae/tv/2006/09/10/
Upper-St-Clair-graduate-writes-for-CBS-s-Jericho/
stories/200609100286).

Peraza, Laura. "Stephen Chbosky on 'Perks.'" World
Book Night US, November 14, 2013. Retrieved
March 28, 2014 (http://www.us.worldbooknight
.org/blog/item/490-stephen-chbosky-on-perks).

Ratcliff, Ashley. "'The Perks of Being' a Filmmaker."
Home Media Magazine, February 12, 2013.
Retrieved March 28, 2014 (http://www
.homemediamagazine.com/summit/perks
-being-filmmaker-29613).

Rosen, Lisa. "The Perks of Being a Novelist."
*Written By: The Journal of the Writers Guild
of America*, September/October 2012.

Sciullo, Maria. "Stephen Chbosky's Latest Work Pays
    Homage to Stephen King." *Pittsburgh Post-
    Gazette*, May 12, 2013. Retrieved April 10, 2014
    (http://www.post-gazette.com/ae/movies/2013/
    05/12/Stephen-Chbosky-latest-work-pays-homage
    -to-Stephen-King/stories/201305120214).
Script Magazine. "Screenwriter and Novelist
    Stephen Chbosky: Rebel with a Cause."
    September 21, 2012. Retrieved March 12, 2014
    (http://www.scriptmag.com/features/writer
    -profiles/screenwriter-noveliststephen-chbosky
    -rebel-with-a-cause-2).
Tapley, Kristopher. "Interview: Stephen Chbosky on
    Pittsburgh Toughness and 'The Perks of Being
    a Wallflower.'" Hitfix.com, September 5, 2012.
    Retrieved April 11, 2014 (http://www.hitfix.com/
    in-contention/interview-stephen-chbosky-on
    -bringing-pittsburgh-toughness-to-the-perks-of
    -being-a-wallflower).
Twitch Film videocast. "The Perks of Being a
    Wallflower Writer/Director Stephen Chbosky."
    September 28, 2012. Retrieved April 7, 2014
    (https://www.youtube.com/watch?v=Ut73oliefNY).
Vancheri, Barbara. "The Perks of Being Stephen
    Chbosky: Upper St. Clair Native Talks About His
    Novel and New Film." *Pittsburgh Post-Gazette*,
    September 26, 2012. Retrieved February 27, 2014

(http://www.post-gazette.com/ae/movies/2012/
09/26/The-perks-of-being-Stephen-Chbosky
-Upper-St-Clair-native-talks-about-his-novel-and
-new-film/stories/201209260184).

Vancheri, Barbara. "Stephen Chbosky Talks 'Perks of
Being a Wallflower' at Manor Today in Pittsburgh."
Pittsburgh Post-Gazette, September 30, 2012.
Retrieved March 29, 2014 (http://blogs.sites.post
-gazette.com.php5-22.dfw1-2.websitetestlink
.com/index.php/arts-a-entertainment?start=171).

ABOUT THE AUTHOR

Philip Wolny is a writer and editor from Queens, New York. His other biographical titles for Rosen Publishing include *Isaac Asimov* (Great Science Writers), *Andrew Mason and Groupon* (Internet Biographies), and *Ludacris* (The Library of Hip-Hop Biographies), among others.

PHOTO CREDITS

Cover, p. 3 JC Olivera/WireImage/Getty Images; p. 7 Leslie Nestor Miranda/FilmMagic/Getty Images; p. 11 Rivers of Steel National Heritage Area; p. 13 Mandel Ngan/AFP/Getty Images; pp. 16–17 Bob Thomas/Popperfoto/Getty Images; pp. 18–19 Archive Photos/MoviePix/Getty Images; pp. 22–23 David McNew/Getty Images; p. 25 Peter Kramer/Getty Images; p. 26 World Book Night; pp. 30–31 © Paramount/ Courtesy Everett Collection; p. 33 Michael Ochs Archives/ Getty Images; p. 37 adapted from biglike/iStock/Thinkstock; pp. 42–43 © AP Images; p. 47 Vers Anderson/WireImage/ Getty Images; p. 49 E. Charbonneau/WireImage/Getty Images; p. 52 Randall Michelson/WireImage/Getty Images; pp. 56, 58–59 CBS Photo Archive/Getty Images; p. 63 Bloomberg/Getty Images; p. 66 Gareth Cattermole/Getty Images; p. 70 Charles Eshelman/FilmMagic/Getty Images; pp. 73, 76–77 John Bramley/© Summit Entertainment/ Courtesy Everett Collection; pp. 74–75 Francois Guillot/ AFP/Getty Images; pp. 80–81 Kevin Winter/Getty Images; p. 83 Matt Sayles/Invision/AP Images; cover, back cover, interior pages (book) © www.istockphoto.com/Andrzej Tokarski; cover, back cover, interior pages (background pattern) javarman/Shutterstock.com; interior pages background image (brick wall) © iStockphoto.com/DRB Images, LLC.

Designer: Nicole Russo;
Executive Editor: Hope Lourie Killcoyne